Nyota Goes Stargazing

Written by Shili Joseph Somi

Illustrated by TullipStudio

Acknowledgments
Maddy Nicole Heeszel, Zita Kamwendo, Salome Thuo, Lucas Jacob, TullipStudio.

DEDICATION

With lots of love to my Wife Sophia and my two Children Julian and Eli. This book is dedicated also to all Swahili learners around the World.

Hi, my name is Nyota.

In Swahili, nyota means star.

My name means star, but I'm a human!
I'm 7-years-old, and I speak Swahili.

Today, I'm going stargazing.

This means I'm going to be looking at the stars in the anga.

Anga means sky.

Do you like looking at the anga for nyota?

If you'd like, you can go stargazing with me!
It would be a lot of fun.
And we could become good friends.
Say marafiki. Marafiki means friends.

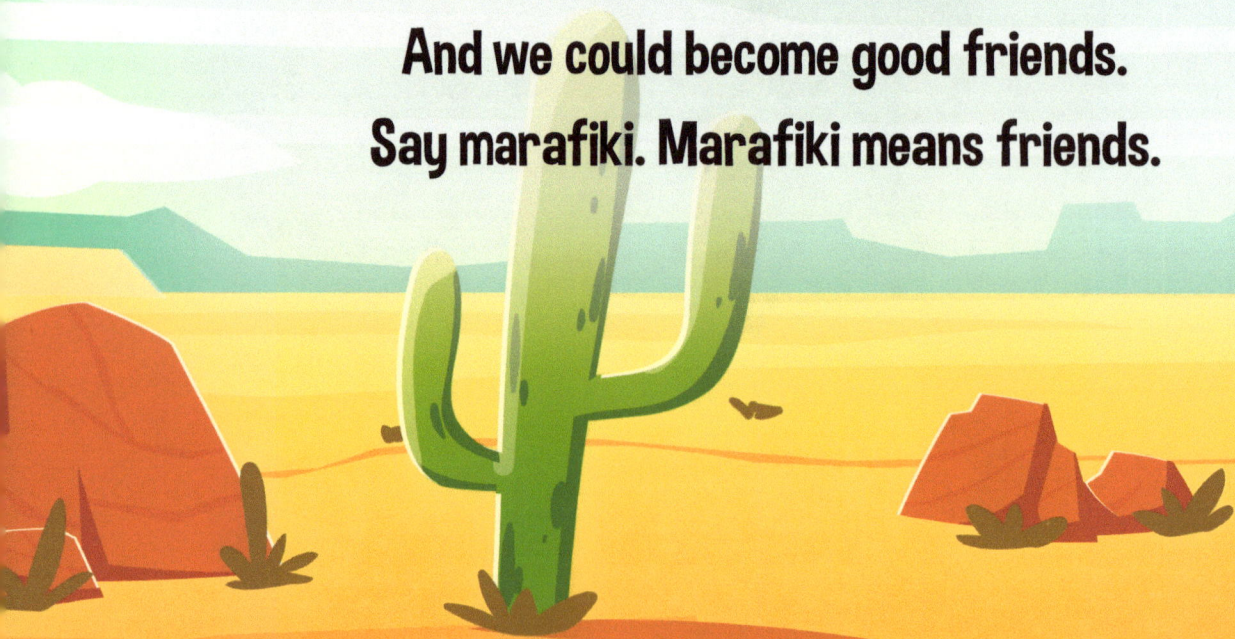

Look at the sky now.

The sun is still setting.

We will have to wait until it gets dark.

Giza means dark in Swahili.

While we're waiting, I'll tell you a secret.
I'm actually afraid of the giza.
But the bright stars make me feel salama.
Salama means safe, by the way.

Hey, look!

I see a star in the sky.

Do you see how it shines like a diamond?

Almasi is diamond in Swahili.

What is your favorite thing about stars?

I love it when they twinkle.

They almost look like they're dancing!

Kucheza means dancing in my language.

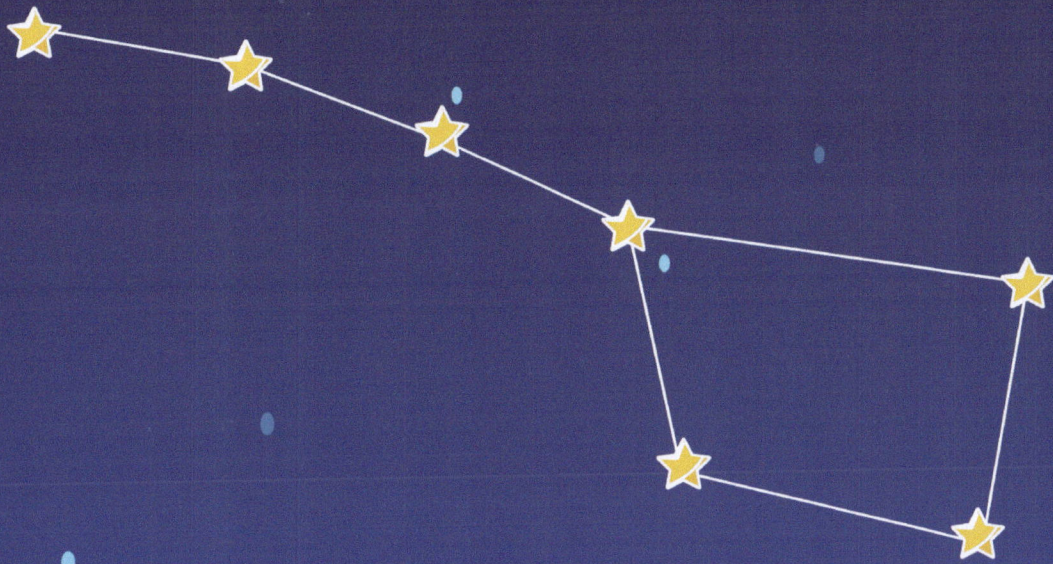

If you look to the left, you will see the Big Dipper.
It kind of looks like a giant spoon.
And there's the Little Dipper!
They're both ajabu, which means wonderful.

You see that star that's moving across the sky?
That's a shooting star.
In Swahili, we call it a kimondo.
They're hard to find!

Have you noticed how stars can be different sizes?

Some are also brighter than others.

That's what makes them unique.

In Swahili, unique is kipekee.

Sometimes I wish it were always nighttime.
There's something so peaceful about stargazing.
Sadly, the stars hide away when the sun is out.
So, we can't see the stars in the daytime.

But did you know that the sun is also a star?

It's the biggest star in our universe!

Say jua.

Wow - you just said sun in Swahili!

Well, it's getting usiku - that means night.

That means it's time for bed.

Thank you for stargazing with me!

I hope you'll watch the nyota again with me soon.

HOW TO INTRODUCE YOURSELF

What is you're name ?	Jina lako ni nani?
My name is	Jina langu ni ....
How old are you?	Una miaka mingapi?
Iam seven years old	Nina miaka Saba
Where are you from?	Unatoka wapi?
I'm from America	Natokea Marekani
You're Nationality ?	Uraia wako?
American Citizen	Raia wa Marekani
Do you speak English ?	Je, unazumgumza Kiingereza?
Yes, I speak English	Ndiyo, ninazungumza Kiingereza
Do you speak Swahili ?	Unazungumza Kiswahili?
Just a little bit	Kidogo tu

GREETINGS/SALAMU

Hello	Jambo/hujambo?
How are you?	Habari yako? /Habari gani?
Fine, thanks	Nzuri, asante
What's up?	Mambo?
Cool	Poa
How are things?	Mambo vipi?
Things are good	Mambo poa
Good morning	Habari za asubuhi?
Good afternoon	Habari za mchana?
Good evening	Habari za jioni?
Nice to meet you	Nimefurahi kukutana na wewe
Also	Pia
Good night	Usiku mwema
Same to you	Na wewe pia
See you later	Tutaonana baadaye
Thank you so much	Asante sana
Goodbye	Kwaheri

COMMON SWAHILI WORDS

Welcome	Karibu
You're most welcome	Karibu sana
Thank you	Asante
Thank you very much	Asante sana
Yes	Ndiyo
No	Hapana
Ok	Sawa
Never mind	Usijali
No problem	Hakuna Shida
No worries	Hakuna matata
Can you help me?	Unaweza kunisaidia?
Yes, I can.	Ndiyo, ninaweza
No, I can't	Hapana, siwezi
No, thank you	Hapana, asante
Why ?	Kwanini?
I don't know	Sijui
When?	Lini
Where?	Wapi
Please	Tafadhari
Excuse me	Samahani
Today	Leo
Now	Sasa
Right now	Sasa hivi
Later	Baadaye
Next time	Siku nyingine

Tomorrow	Kesho
Yesterday	Jana
Day before yesterday	Juzi
Day after tomorrow	Kesho kutwa
Day	Siku
Time	Muda
Minutes	Dakika
Seconds	Sekunde
Food	Chakula
Tea	Chai
Coffee	Kahawa
Sugar	Sukari
Salt	Chumvi
Water	Maji
Father	Baba
Mother	Mama
Grandma	Bibi
Grandpa	Bibi
Uncle	Mjomba
Aunt	Shangazi
Brother	Kaka
Sister	Dada
Child	Mtoto
Girl	Msichana
Boy	Mvulana
Woman	Mwanamke
Man	Mwanaume

About the Author:

Shili Joseph Somi is the author ,founder and CEO of swahiliprime. He is a husband, and father of two boys .He is very passionate of promoting Swahili language and African Cultures.

The idea of starting swahiliprime came after he discovered that many immigrant's kids have difficulties in learning /speaking their mother language while growing up in a foreign country .They face a language barrier especially when they visit their motherland .

With swahiliprime we are committed to educate and enlighten learners in a way that they can retain information while having fun at the same time.

www.swahiliprime.com

Instagram | Facebook | Youtube | Twitter @swahiliprime

www.ingramcontent.com/pod-product-compliance
Lightning Source LLC
Chambersburg PA
CBHW041244040426
42445CB00005B/143